THIS BOOK
BELONGS TO

_____

_____

_____

_____

_____

Kindly return if found

RECIPE
for
PRESS

PITCH YOUR STORY LIKE
THE PROS & CREATE A BUZZ

by **AMY FLURRY**

featuring
Hugh Acheson
Amy Butler
David Butler
Rebecca Wood
Kara Larson
Sonja Rasula

PC
Press

Published by PC Press
Atlanta, GA
Printed in the United States
by Progress Printing Plus
10 9 8 7 6 5 4 3 2 1

First Edition
ISBN: 978-0-9846089-8-0

INTRODUCTION

As a freelance writer and editor who spent the last 18 years telling other people's stories, I often thought that if I had a product, I would use the power of press to spread the word. Instead of advertising, I'd invest my time in personalizing pitches, identifying and approaching the right editors and maintaining a constant presence across their desks. After all, press is free if you can get it!

But that's easy for me to say. I know what a good pitch looks like and how to win over an editor in an email. I know the key to getting an influential blogger in Hong Kong to consider covering a product. I know the small communication gaffes that undermine your chance of scoring press. And I know that you don't need a publicist to secure local, region even national placements.

But DIY publicity is unfamiliar territory for most. Owners often think that press is only for the people who can afford an expensive PR firm. And they may go on thinking this until, by chance, an editor or freelance writer covers their business (I was the author of first-time articles for many). After seeing it's powerful impact on traffic and sales, one question predictably follows. "How can I get more?"

The rules of the publicity game are changing. With online publications significantly speeding up the press to publication deadlines, exclusives and scoops are harder to come by. Editors aren't choosy about the messenger. They're more eager to secure a new story, a new product or even a new angle on an established brand and get it into production fast. Editors simply want to work with people who know how to work with them.

I wrote *Recipe for Press* to give you these tools and the insider insight to approach editors and expect results.

But I also wrote it because I believe that establishing an in-house communications team and managing your publicity from the inside—even if it starts with just you—is critical to whether your company will exist five to ten years from now.

Plenty of great products with passionate people behind them fail, whereas others with so-so services receive the bulk of the attention. The difference isn't luck; the difference is what you will find in the pages of *Recipe for Press*.

Never before have their been so many outlets for sharing your story. Today's media landscape is not just about being featured in *O* magazine, it's about being a new entry on Oh Joy! blog. It is as easy to land a placement in an online Australian magazine as it is a story in a local newspaper.

And no longer are these placements reserved, as it once seemed, for designers and brands in New York alone. Editors and writers are just as eager to cover the small outfit in Florence, Alabama or the Portland, Oregon birdhouse operation as they are a new Target collaboration, as long as they believe you are prepared for the attention and treat press as an integral arm of the business. If you don't navigate this course with skill and a strategy, writers simply move on to someone else with a story to tell, or a product to sell who "gets it."

Having been on the receiving end of decades of press releases, pitches and products, I know—at a glance— what makes them successful. And I have long wanted to share it. As a freelance writer, I am a pro at extracting a handful of story ideas from one interview, and it's going to be a lot of fun to teach you how. I remember back to my college days, however, when professors of some of my journalism classes seemed so far out of touch from the material they taught.

In 2010, I introduced a product into the marketplace with a friend called Paper-Cut-Project. We make one of the most non-saleable items possible to dream up: paper styling props for high-end fashion productions. With nothing but imagination and know-how, we have pitched our work to editors and bloggers here and abroad, and from these placements companies including Hermès, Cartier, Kate Spade and The Bay have found us and commissioned collection after collection. We have not only enjoyed a surprising amount of success, we've depended on this method to share our story with a very exclusive market. And if there's one thing I've learned, one story doesn't cut it in order for the right people to find us. We need a constant brand presence across a number of different print and online outlets to really make the difference.

DIY publicity may seem like a daunting endeavor, at first. But you'll find that there's something very familiar and comforting about it's core. Positive press comes from relationships that you create with editors and writers and bloggers who are as passionate about their work as you are your own. My hope is that *Recipe for Press* brings an energizing new degree of insight and creativity to your publicity efforts.

A very special thank you to Gemma, Tony, Melissa, Shannon, Caroline, Lidia and Alan for helping me see this through. And to Camille and Ellis who keep me going.

Table of Contents

one

WHO ARE YOU?

You think you have a story to tell or a product worth sharing and that is why you picked up this book. I know you have something to say because I have made a wonderful career telling those of others like you.

In fact, you have a lot in common with competitors who get all of the press. You've both taken risks to put a business in place, perhaps even snubbed your nose at good sense and conventionality to see it through. You've even turned a passion into profit on some level.

So why do some seem to get all of the attention and how can you join the club? Simple: you learn to share the sliver of your story that matters to the editor of the publication or author behind the blog you pitch.

Who are you? What do you like to do? How does it relate to your company? Perhaps most importantly, why did you choose the place you hope to see your story featured?

Writers develop original content and find angles by spending time with their subjects. The longer we listen and the better our questions, the more ideas we can extract from an interview.

But if a writer isn't knocking on your door, then you must get the story to them and do your best to anticipate the angle that would interest them most. Get in the habit of thinking like an editor and recognizing the many stories-within-your-story. There is no shortage of places to publish them, but editors don't all want to run the same thing. They want a new spin on it. The point of a pitch is to narrow the story down to the idea that matters to that editor most.

The next time you're in the magazine section of a bookstore, take a look at the incredible variety of publications on the stands. There are sections devoted to gardening, traveling, knitting, DIY design, tattoos, fashion, architecture.

Spend an hour following the blog rolls of your favorite online magazines and you'll observe an even greater labyrinth of micro-niches.

The trick to seeing your brand featured is in the hook. How do you relate your story to the reader of the publication you are pitching?

A great exercise to help get you there and think outside of the box of your brand is to map the many aspects of who you are. Interview yourself or sit with a friend and, together, chart everything you are, everything you love, and everything you do, in and outside of work. Now practice making your product newsworthy based on this information.

Let's say, for example, you own a neighborhood nail spa with a retail section in the store where you sell nail polishes and gift items like umbrellas, journals, and beauty products. You have a daughter and together you enjoy walking to school each day and lunches with friends, one of whom is recently engaged. A good publicist would use these to tease out leads for your spa story.

Here are a few:
- BANISH THE PALL OF A RAINY DAY WITH A CHEERY PRINTED UMBRELLA.
- KICK THE WINTER DOLDRUMS WITH THE SEASON'S BRIGHT NEW LACQUERS IN POPPY, PERSIMMON AND TANGERINE.
- MANI-PEDI AND A FRIEND: THE NEW COCKTAIL HOUR!
- MOMMY'S NEW LOW-COST ESCAPE.
- TYING THE KNOT: NEW NAIL TRENDS ON EVERY WOMAN'S BIG DAY.

Now take this a step further and look to those who work for you. At a moment when customers are very eager to get a peak behind the curtain to feel a part of your brand family, your employees extend the scope of your audience and how they relate to your product. You'll want to shine the press spotlight on them too and tie their interests back around to your story.

Understanding what makes something newsworthy will help you develop a good story angle and a solid pitch.

Meet Chloe: A Case Study

Chloe is an emerging designer with a new collection and a few
celebrity clients. She is also a vegetarian, a single mother and dance
fanatic who competes in salsa competition on the weekends. She
lives in a mod, loft apartment in Paris, Texas that she decorated
with mid-century modern pieces culled from her favorite downtown vintage shops. She has a six-year-old daughter and a pound
puppy named Violet and she created a child-sitting co-op along with
other entrepreneurial single moms in her community. She loves to
garden and only six months ago spearheaded a push to create a garden to supplement the lunches at her child's elementary school. She
collects vintage chain mesh purses by Whiting & Davis and has
built a surprisingly successful side business selling them on eBay.

Where does our fictitious Chloe's story belong? From the
information presented only in the paragraph above, she could
potentially land placements in magazines including *Dwell*, *Vegetarian
Times*, *Delta Sky*, *Whole Dog Journal*, *Bust*, *Working Woman*, *Paper City*
(Texas Edition), *Self*, *Cooking Light*, *Redbook*, *Whole Woman*, *Texas*,
Garden & Gun, *Southern Living*, *Elle*, *Better Homes & Gardens*, *Nylon*,
Glamour, and countless online publications.

News can be generated or tied to a hobby, a location, a recent
study, a current event, a season or holiday. Understanding what
makes news— from an editors viewpoint— will help you develop
a good story angle and a solid pitch.

two

ANTICIPATING STORIES

*Thinking like an
editor can help
you anticipate
what a magazine
will be looking
for and how
future issues
will be shaped.*

*B*efore working up a pitch it's a good idea to get to know the publications you'd like to be featured in. Reading a few back issues will give you a clear sense of whether your story or product is right for that magazine or blog. The goal is to identify not one but perhaps a few sections of the publication where your brand makes sense, where a placement would have the most impact. If you are a professional organizer with your own line of closet containers, for example, you could potentially be featured in a story on time management or quoted as an expert. If your goal is to sell a particular product or to generate web traffic then your best bet may be to pitch something new from your product line. You might title your pitch… **Curbing Closet Clutter, a bold new product that makes life a little easier.** It's possible an editor would use your title, and then include your piece within the product roundup or showcase, a win-win for you and the editor.

My point is that if you study back issues of a publication and their online components, you'll start to see patterns in how content is featured. It also becomes easier to identify where there is room for you to insert new ideas, to break in. The same is true for blogs; most have an established format. Your job is to anticipate what editors will be looking for and where there's room to plug in your story or product. When you take the time to study back issues, identifying the right fit gets easier and really betters your chance of getting the editor's attention.

Woman's Day, for example, is a women's service magazine a la *Family Circle, Redbook* and *Good Housekeeping* and among the largest subscription based magazines in the country. With a focus on traditional values of home, family and children, their monthly lineup generally includes stories on time management, organizing, financial planning, cleaning, parenting and health. These themes haven't changed much in the last 20 years but the story angles are made modern each month. A spring-cleaning story then, for example, may have been titled, "Spring Cleaning Simplified: Ten easy steps." Today's spring cleaning story reads, "How to Green Your Spring Cleaning Routine," with a sidebar showcasing the latest eco-friendly products that work as well as your old favorites.

One of the greatest resources for anyone looking to break into a magazine is the editorial calendar. This is a schedule of editorial themes for each issue and it is usually posted under the media kit link in the advertising section of the magazine's website. By now we can anticipate that April will be the "Green" issue for many magazines and that pitching ideas and products for Valentine's Day gift guides will be right for February. But when you know that a magazine's July issue will be their "Restaurant and Dining" issue, or that the May issue has a "Bargain" focus, then you can craft and time your pitches accordingly.

IDEA BOX

Do you still have stacks of now-defunct favorites like *Domino, Cookie, ReadyMade, Men's Vogue* or *O @ Home?* With pages of great material that are still relevant or can be tweaked to make current, they're excellent sources for ideas that can kick-start a pitch.

Even the smallest effort to tie a pitch into longstanding themes or to put a clever and new spin on predictable headliners goes a long way with an editor, showing that you are well versed with the magazine or blog and that you have made some effort to understand what they are looking for.

MEET HUGH ACHESON

In my 18 years as a freelance writer, a few subjects who have really made it on the national scene, stand out for the ease of working together. Despite a high profile and crazed schedule— turnaround on questions, phone calls and emails will be quick and the experience a pleasure. Hugh Acheson, a five-time James Beard Foundation Award nominee for Best Chef in the Southeast, has long put a priority on press, though he's never hired a publicist. In valuing editorial as a key ingredient in getting word out about his restaurants, he single-handedly put a small Southern college town on the culinary map with his first fine dining establishment, Five &Ten in Athens, Georgia. Adding two more restaurants to his regional roster—The National, also in Athens and Empire State South in Atlanta—he continues to cultivate relationships with editors and writers and educates his staff on how to do the same. With a new role as a judge on Bravo's hit cooking show, *Top Chef,* and a new book, *A New Turn in the South: Southern Flavors Reinvented For Your Kitchen* (Clarkson Potter), Hugh and his growing in-house team keep writers and editors interested by being pro-active. Here's how, over the years, he's fostered those relationships and anticipated editor's needs.

YOU MENTIONED THAT YOU KEEP IDEAS AND RECIPES "AT THE READY" FOR EDITORS. HOW HAS THAT HELPED YOUR BUSINESS?

HUGH ACHESON: I learned a long time ago that sometimes editors are looking for content at the last minute and if I could turn around a request quickly then I would be sure to get the press and also high on their list of people they would call the next time a food article was being written. We keep a couple of seasonal menus and some recipes at the ready, changing the stash every once in a while to keep it current. Sometimes we have to curate to a more specific request, but often the content that we have prepared is more than enough. We are fast content providers!

QUESTION *and* ANSWER
HUGH ACHESON
hughacheson.com • chef /author

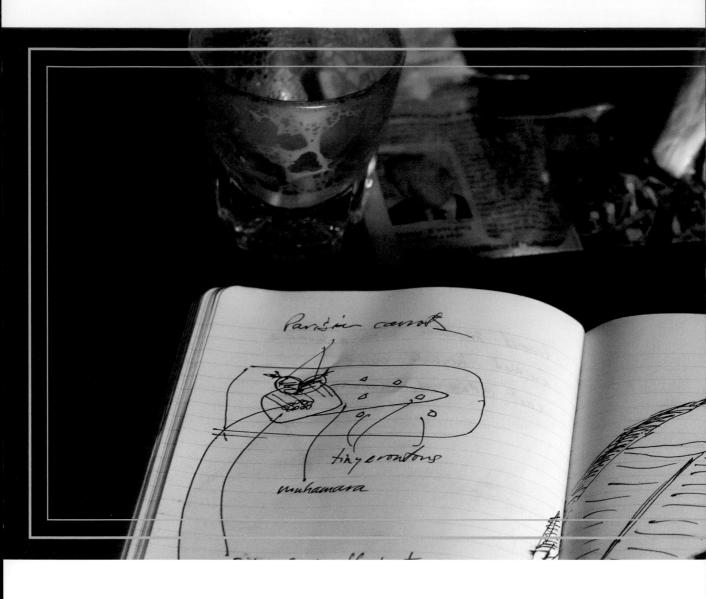

HOW DID YOU KNOW TO MAKE PRESS A PRIORITY?

HA: I worked for a chef once who was brutally honest about getting press. "They (the magazines) just want to get the article done, so if they ask you for a recipe, drop everything and write it and send it, same day!" He was correct in assuming that most chefs would procrastinate on getting the content back to the publication, or just completely forget as they got busy with their regular routine. Being responsive, kind, thoughtful and punctual has served us very well when it comes to getting press.

Acheson keeps a notebook within easy reach so he can jot down a potential article idea or draw a quick sketch. "I find if I can remind myself of the initial idea I am much more likely to nurture it into a real concept."

AFTER SO MANY YEARS IN THE BUSINESS, HOW DO YOU NOW ANTICIPATE WHAT EDITORS OR BLOGGERS MAY NEED?

HA: We look at trends and try to stay current in our food thought process. The core of what we do— Southern food and local food— has been very popular in the last decade and that has helped a lot. It would be harder if what we did was just fondue.

HOW DO YOU PREPARE?

HA: We read and watch trends. We look through the blogs of others we like, we read books that are newly released, we eat at other restaurants. We travel and react to what is real and beautiful. I am a simple practitioner at heart so I strive for honesty and beauty in food, not for the novel and fantastic. That would make it much harder to achieve success every day.

DO YOU PITCH IDEAS TO EDITORS OR WAIT FOR THEM TO COME TO YOU?

HA: I have a small core group that I work closely with: my assistant Lauren Johnson, wine director Steve Grubbs, my fellow chef partners Chuck Ramsey, Peter Dale, Ryan Smith and a couple of others. I bounce ideas off them and we chat about concepts before we ever put an idea in front of an editor. I would say one of 20 gets sea legs and the others get tossed. Too many ideas can muddy the core of what you do. Sometimes ideas are more attractive to the press than the consumer, regardless of amount of press. This is very apparent in our "Tiffin Lunch Program" which is a multi-tiered lunch box, which people would take to their desks to have an elaborate picnic there. Because of the deposit on the tiffin, they have not flown off the shelf but the press loves writing about them! They are very cute and current.

DID YOU INVEST IN A GOOD CAMERA FOR DIY ACTION SHOTS OR DO YOU BUDGET FOR PHOTO SHOOTS?

HA: We have a good Nikon and our iPhones, but would rather our skilled friends who are photographers do their thing, so that we have great images to support the ideas. We found that is a smart investment, as often publications use the photos we supply.

HAVE YOU EVER HAD A PUBLICIST FOR YOUR RESTAURANTS?

HA: We have never paid for PR. It was never in our budget. We found that people like dealing directly with us so we took care of it on our own. And contrary to popular belief, restaurants don't make piles of money so we have to think about the bottom line.

ARE THERE THINGS YOU DO TO MAKE IT EASIER FOR PRESS TO WORK WITH YOU?

HA: Get it finished. Completing projects feels good. Impress people with your ability to do it faster and better than most.

three

PITCH
PERFECT

What makes a successful pitch? Tone, brevity, creativity, polish and a good photo, for starters. I receive hundreds of pitches a month and they come in all shapes and sizes, but there is one format that will get full consideration every time.

A great pitch is one created specifically for the individual on the receiving end. Gone are the days of boring press releases that run on and on about a new product or company without making the case for why it would work for the publication or the editor being approached. But a tightly focused, personalized pitch with a zinger of a headline or lead will make an editor want to read further and consider.

Get to know the publication you are pitching. Identifying a possible fit is the first step to placing the story and your conviction, confidence and purpose will resonate in a well-written pitch.

There are several components that an editor needs to see in a pitch (and we'll cover them all.) But it is important to remember that you are laying the foundation of a relationship with the editor. The pitch with potential will reveal that you have done your research.

If your pitch is presented in a way that reflects you have put time and thought into crafting the query, an editor will give careful consideration to consecutive appeals, even if they have to pass on the one in front of them. But hurling ideas haphazardly or submitting simultaneous queries to every editor you know with hopes that something will stick is, ultimately, more detrimental to your press efforts than productive.

WHAT DOES A GOOD PITCH LOOK LIKE?

Editors today prefer to receive a pitch by email, so save the postage! Do make sure you state the intent of the email in the subject header, being as specific and inviting as possible. For example, if the pitch is for the Healthy Living section of the magazine, say so in the email subject like this: New product/Healthy Living section.

Always address an editor or blogger by name. If you don't bother to find out who you should approach, then the editor on the receiving end won't feel at all obligated to read it. If you give a writer or an editor a reason to believe they are part of a mass email blast it is all the easier for them to delete.

A successful magazine pitch will answer the following basic questions and will do so in two to three solid paragraphs. A pitch to a blogger can be substantially shorter, but needs to be equally compelling.

Who are you?	Short Introduction
What's the big idea?	Strong Lead
When did it launch?	Relevance To The Issue You Are Pitching
Why does it matter?	Unique Feature(s) That Set Your Product Apart
Where does it belong?	Specific Section Of The Magazine
How do I learn more?	Contact Details, Website, Price

Brevity and strong photography is key to cracking online and print publications. Editors are extremely visual people. They can usually determine if they want to learn more based on a glance at the lead and the photo you submit. If they connect to the picture and your hard-to-resist title or lead, then they'll likely read the e-mail and consider the unique features you've presented, like a local economic angle, a green message or a celebrity customer. If they're still interested, editors will then visit your website.

Great photographs help a pitch rise to the top of the submissions pile, so choose images that look like they could be plugged directly into the page or blog you're pitching. The pictures should be low resolution (72 dpi) and embedded directly into the email for easy viewing. Editors won't open attachments unless they have requested the images.

Writing the perfect pitch is like composing a pop song. You need a catchy title and a chorus or hook that is easy to remember. It seems like it should be the easiest thing in the world to write, but it actually takes time and a very deliberate approach to find that sweet spot.

CRAFTING AN IRRESISTIBLE PITCH

A strong pitch doesn't run on and on. As editors are increasingly swamped with blind, impersonal submissions, they prefer you approach them with only a few paragraphs, supported with a great product shot or picture. Still, one of the best ways to sell your idea is by giving the pitch an attention-grabbing title that introduces the pitch and helps the editor visualize what it is you're proposing. Here's an example of a compelling pitch with everything an editor needs to give it proper consideration.

• •

Fun, Local Alternative to Screen Overload

Dear Catherine,

Several of your recent columns talked about the struggle for parents to limit the time their kids spend in front of computer, television and video screens. Six months ago I opened Firefly, a children's shop in downtown Abilene, Texas with the purpose of giving them an engaging outlet for play. This week we launched our website and posted a calendar of new classes, include beginner's knitting! And because the site is e-commerce ready, parents everywhere can shop for puzzles, books and toys that are great for creative play. I would love for you to introduce Firefly to your readers or select a product from our new online shop to run in your Editor's Picks page of the magazine.

I've included a picture, below, of one of our best-selling art kits and I am happy to provide high-resolution images of the store or other product upon request. Our website is: Fireflyloveskids.com. Thank you so much for your time and consideration.

Amy Flurry
Amy@fireflyloveskids.com
706-555-1234

• •

Use back issues of the magazine as a guide when working up an angle or story idea and notice the formulas in place that you might plug in to.

THE PITCH CHECKLIST

Before hitting the send button, make sure your pitch can answer the questions below. You want to make it easy for the writer to fully understand your story and why it is relevant to their readers.

Do you have an exciting hook that connects it to the publication's readers?

Did you demonstrate some simple familiarity with the blog or magazine by specifying the specific section you are pitching?

Have you mentioned what makes the idea timely?

Have you offered the editor an extra incentive, like an exclusive image, to write about you or your company's product?

Did you double-check the spelling of the editor's or blogger's name?

Did you include your website and contact number?

Did you mention that you have high-resolution images available upon request?

four

THE IMPORTANCE OF BEING NEW

THE **IMPORTANCE** OF BEING **NEW**

NEW & IMPROVED

HOTTEST NEWEST LATEST

NEW ADDRESS New Menu

MORE / *n o w*

TRENDSPOTTING

Fresh Picks

new color

NEW

FIRST BITES & NOW

LATEST

cutting

edge *what's* *new*

brand new

SCOOP

WHAT TO EAT RIGHT NOW

NEW STYLE

NEW & IMPROVED

HOTTEST NEWEST LATEST

Fresh Picks **NEW**

NEW FIRST BITES & NOW

& NOW *TRENDSPOTTING*

*E*ditors are chasing one thing: the next new thing! We want to be the first to try it, the first to share with our audience, the first to report on it.

"New" is the currency of media, it's what drives the publishing industry each month and it's why more and more brands from beauty to fashion to office supply stagger product releases. Because each new offering presents a fresh opportunity for press, this slow rollout strategy takes advantage of the myriad of opportunities and outlets, to squeeze the most publicity of one collection or season.

Of course the best time to capitalize on easy press is when your company is, in fact, new. As obvious as this may sound, it's a step that many neglect in the busy lead up to opening their doors. I've seen so many store owners sign contracts with publicists in the first weeks after opening because business was slower than anticipated. They realized, too late, that they neglected an important facet of their own grand opening: extending an invitation to press.

Public relations firms typically charge between three and ten thousand dollars a month and require a minimum six-month contract. That money could be better invested in an in-house communications position that will grow your brand. Even at this stage, it's not too late for you to build a buzz by approaching bloggers and online editors who work on very short lead times.

From there it's up to you to attract press around things that are "new" to the brand like events, program launches, a warehouse sale, a second location, a collaboration, a website redesign, a new staff member, and so on. Think strategically and develop a calendar of ideas and who you plan to pitch. And always be sure you have strong photos to support your news.

NEW? LET ME COUNT THE WAYS!

The easiest place to break into most magazines (and the sections with the most opportunities for new faces/brands) is the front of the magazines. These pages, referred to as 'front-of-book' by editors, generally make up the first section of editorial just after the masthead (see Chapter Six) and editor's letter. Each page features four to five tidbits of timely news. The names of these sections— fresh picks, trend spotting, hot list, first bites— usually suggest that this space is reserved for right-now news, and the editor who compiles these pages is generally listed on the first or last page of that section.

What are they looking for? These sections are dedicated to "news flash" items, timely information that may not be, on its own, enough for a feature story, but still warrant attention and send the reader into action.

Do you have a new e-commerce shop? Then title the pitch, "A new way to shop an old favorite." Giving an editor the hook is a good way to convince them it is news that readers need to know now! Have you moved your boutique or artist's collective to a hip new part of town? Then your lead should play up the fact that you are the latest addition to an emerging neighborhood for the city's best indie shopping. If your longstanding brand has new packaging, don't neglect to include a picture of a label when you share this old favorite's new look. A new calorie counting app presents an opportunity to entice an editor and engage readers with the best new mobile device for staying fit. Will your store carry a new clothing line that shoppers in your city can only find there? Then you have a regional exclusive on your hands. If the latest addition to your existing line of umbrellas happens to be the runway's newest "it" shade, connect those dots to make it new! A trunk show with a visiting designer? Ballet performance with special guest artist? These are the kind of newsworthy items that pepper the front-of-book pages, the section of the magazines where editors are most open to entertaining ideas from newcomers.

You'll have more success when you pitch these fertile grounds and you'll establish with that editor that you know what you're doing. Nothing says "out of their league" than a newcomer who pitches an idea for a feature story when it's not even developed enough to be considered for a front of the magazine item.

A WEBSITE THAT WORKS

Once you have the attention of an editor, you can bet that the first place they visit is your website if they're interested in learning more. Editors will know whether or not your brand fits their publication almost upon first glance, so be sure that the website reflects your best before reaching out.

Editors need to feel comfortable in sending their readers to your site and confident that you can handle the attention and traffic. If you site is still under construction or if the current aesthetic isn't the one you want to communicate, wait until it is press-ready to contact an editor. And if you have a product, be sure you have a shopping cart or can direct editors to a site where readers can go to purchase it.

NEW STYLE

NEW PATTERN

NEW COLOR

NEW SCENT

five

THE POWER
OF THE PICTURE

Good photography is the single most important component in communicating your brand to today's media influencers and it greatly affects whether or not they share your story with their audience.

A good picture can elevate a product and help you break into a new market. It also gives you the edge on a competitor. If an editor, for example, is forced to choose between two products they like equally, they will consistently choose the one with good print-ready images. Why? For many magazines, budgets for editorial productions are at an all-time low. If an editor can use what you provide instead of shooting it themselves, it simply helps them stay within budget.

Bloggers post content more frequently and almost always use the images provided to them. So it makes sense that the most direct path to their hearts and pages is in submitting great pictures.

Where should you look for a photographer who can deliver editorial-friendly pictures? One savvy way is to check out the photographer credits in strong regional or city magazines and blogs. Look for the photo credits and then visit their personal website. Study their portfolio and client lists to see if their experience and style matches your needs.

Capable photographers can also be found through local design schools, art institutes or college graduate programs. Students are always looking for ways to build their portfolio, to gain experience, and they may be more affordable than a working photographer. Still, it's a good idea to discuss your needs with a curriculum director and ask for a reference before hiring. Remember, the goal is to create images that can be used by editors, and there is a huge gulf between a pretty picture and a press-ready photograph. Be wary of photographers who want to over-style. Crisp, well-lit product shots against a white backdrop are more desirable over elaborately styled presentations any day.

It is still smart to invest in a good digital camera to take pictures and create content for your social media sites and your blog, where candid photography and unstaged, behind-the-scenes snapshots are appropriate.

Coming into your brand's style is a creative process, one that will evolve over time. Pictures bear witness to new discovery and inspirations; they document these new chapters of your story.

Your story extends beyond photography, of course. It is every ingredient that makes up the brand ratatouille: the company name, the logo, the studio, the fabulous employees. But pictures tell your story for you when you're not there to deliver it yourself. They communicate a lifestyle and ultimately they sell a product that people may not be able to touch or hold in person.

Few brands communicate their philosophy and lifestyle better or more consistently than Amy Butler. I was introduced to Amy and her husband David Butler fifteen years ago. She was a contributing editor to *Country Living* and I was among the magazine's stable of writers and producers. My assignment was a six-page spread featuring the couples' Granville, Ohio home. *Country Living* often turned the spotlight on their contributors who lived the lifestyle the magazine proffered.

At that time Amy had just launched a line of fabric and used her home as a set for staging photo shoots for various products and projects. David, whose multidisciplinary design studio, Art of the Midwest, teamed with Amy for her graphics, also photographed new collections and lifestyle images that support a look they coined "Midwest Modern."

Now in her 20th year, Amy Butler, the brand, has an international following with enviable partnerships including a line of quilting fabrics and organic yarns for ROWAN, wallpapers for Graham & Brown, an eco-friendly stationary line and recent book, *Amy Butler's Midwest Modern.*

Collection after collection she delivers visuals that help tell the story of the crisp, graphic-driven prints and the inspirations that inform them, like nature's vibrant and oft-dueling color waves. Trends may change, but the look and feel of Amy Butler's designs over the years has remained uniquely her own.

Here's what they have to say about the roll of photography in building and promoting a brand.

YOU SPENT A NUMBER OF YEARS AS A MAGAZINE EDITOR. HOW HAS THAT EXPERIENCE CARRIED OVER IN PROMOTING YOUR OWN BRAND?

AMY BUTLER: I think I learned about continuity, about making sure that someone can follow the "bigger picture" all the way down to detail shots. It helps to make sense of what you are looking at so that the idea comes together on different levels within the shoot. It's a narrative that weaves the story together through imagery; you want to make sure that it makes sense.

DO YOU USE ONLY DIGITAL PRESS KITS AT THIS POINT?

AB: I don't use the traditional press kits that many businesses use. I try to keep my communication with our press contacts more personal. I send out emails to our key press contacts to announce new products or any news from the studio. I try to keep the message to the point including all the pertinent information, a few photos, links to my website where they can learn more and easy to use contact information. Since I usually only send one to three images per announcement it is even more important that the images convey the message we want to show. Editors are extremely busy and they receive dozens of product pitches every day. Sending a personal note with a quick overview of my new product stands out from the multiple pages of press kits that they receive every day.

HOW IMPORTANT IS PHOTOGRAPHY TO COMMUNICATING YOUR STORY?

AB: Very, very important! Photography is really key because through our images I'm able to tell a story about each product or collection in a way that's inspirational and emotive. I have a creative business so I get to be creative with the way I present myself. With blogs and social media you never know where your images will pop up and magazines only have limited space for each product that they feature so it is important that you can tell your story with each image you produce and give them something unique and fresh each time.

BETWEEN YOUR BLOG, VIDEOS AND LOOK BOOK, HOW DO YOU KEEP UP WITH THE DEMAND FOR SO MUCH NEW CONTENT?

AB: There is a lot of post-production organizing with our images. David usually shoots 3,000 – 5,000 images during a photo shoot and then we cut it down to our favorite 200 – 300 images. This is no easy task! After we have our top picks we filter them down even more into various groups and then I cull this group down to my top 20-30 choices. Since I often work with our licensing partner's PR companies, we need enough images for everyone to use. We often organize the images into two groups, one for our bank of images for press and promotions and one for the other PR company to use. This way we are not sending out the same images to each magazine and blog that contacts us.

DO EDITORS GENERALLY USE YOUR PICTURES OR DO THEY PREFER TO SHOOT THE PRODUCT IN THEIR STUDIO?

AB: There is a mix of both and depends on the magazine and what they are using the product for. Many times one of my products, such as a rug, will be called in to be part of a room shot so they need the actual product. Other times they are doing a special mention of a product or fabric collection and we can send them a variety of images from our photography so they can choose one that works best with their magazine and layout.

IS THIS ALSO PART OF YOUR STRATEGY IN CONTROLLING THE BRAND IMAGE?

AB: Definitely! This is so important when trying to establish a brand. It is always fun to see how different publications use my products in their photography but being able to send my own photography ensures that the story I wanted the product to tell is exactly what the reader will see when looking at the publication. This is also true for other press outlets like blogs and other websites. Each website or blog is so different with various styles of writing and how they feature each post. It's nice to always be sure your story is told no matter where it is being published.

HOW DO YOU DECIDE WHAT YOU NEED FOR EACH NEW COLLECTION?

AB: This changes a little bit depending on which collection or product I am shooting. I partner with other companies for many of my products so each group often has different needs. Overall we always do a lifestyle photo shoot for each collection. This tells the story of the collection and the brand and these images are used for everything from my website, the licensing company's website, press information, trade communications and publications to consumer media, blogs and social networking sites. These images can't be specific to one type of publication or audience; they have to appeal to everyone.

I do use straightforward product shots against a white background at times. This type of image is usually used in brochures put together by my licensing partners for trade shows and press kits. These are almost never used alone though, we always intersperse the lifestyle images alongside the straightforward images to show the whole story of the collection and the brand.

I also shoot straightforward images of the sewn samples created at my studio. I put these on my website as inspiration for sewers to see the different ways to combine various fabrics. Since we often continue to create samples after the photo shoot is over for trade shows and our trunk show program, this allows me to share additional inspirational images for consumers and retailers to view. It's a good way for people to see the details and the combinations of prints on each sample.

WHAT ARE YOU DOING TODAY BY WAY OF PHOTOGRAPHY THAT YOU DIDN'T NEED FIVE YEARS AGO?

AB: Well, we're shooting more images than we used to! With the countless number of blogs and various social networking sites you want to be sure there is enough of a variety of images of your product that people are not seeing the exact same shot over and over again on every website or in every magazine. I try to set up different scenarios for different products so there is a diversity of images to choose from.

I also have started to shoot more behind the scenes photos to share with blogs and on my own website and I have had some great feedback on these images; people love to see how everything is put together. Along with the behind the scenes photos we've started shooting short videos during our photo shoots as well. I post these on my website and share with other blogs and press outlets. People love to see what's really going on in the studio and who is involved. It's fun because while David is shooting with the big camera, I can actually walk around and shoot my snaps, sometimes over his shoulder!

"Photography is really key because through our images I'm able to tell a story about each product or collection in a way that's inspirational and emotive."

-AMY BUTLER

DO YOU HAVE A SYSTEM FOR ORGANIZING SO MANY IMAGES?

AB: Having a good organization system is key. If a magazine requests an image from a specific collection it is so easy to pull up the file with the coordinating images rather than searching through the thousands of images we have for the brand. We also have our photography organized into "favorites," this way our top picks are right at our fingertips whenever there is a new press request.

This is also very important because magazines run on very tight deadlines. I often get requests from editors and they need information and an image by the end of the day or within a few hours. If the photography wasn't organized and ready to go I would miss out on important press opportunities all the time.

HOW MUCH OF YOUR BUDGET TO YOU ALLOT FOR PHOTOGRAPHY?

AB: I don't have a strict percentage or dollar amount for each photo shoot, it varies by product and licensing partner. I evaluate each collection and decide how many days are needed and if models are needed. I then decide what type of props and wardrobe we will need and if we need to rent a location. Then there is compensation for the photographer, stylist and assistant used during the shoot. Sometimes I can fit an entire collection into one day, other products need two to three days to shoot. There is always a lot of planning and we try to work out a budget independently for each shoot once I know all of the elements that will be involved.

WHAT LESSONS HAVE YOU LEARNED WHEN IT COMES TO PHOTOGRAPHY THAT READERS MIGHT AVOID?

AB: I try to look at any mistakes as learning opportunities for future projects. They're an important part of the process. More is more, with digital photography. There is no reason to not shoot as many images as you can. Shoot more than you will ever need, experiment with lighting, angles, props and anything else you can imagine. If it doesn't work out you can just delete it later, no extra cost to you. This is also helpful with technology these days. We have had photo shoots where an entire memory card somehow got erased after a shoot. Luckily we shoot thousands of images so although we lost some we still had plenty to choose from without rescheduling an entire day of a shoot.

Prep and organization before the shoot even starts is also key. Having lists and a schedule will help everything go smoothly and greatly reduce stress!

"Shoot more than you will ever need, experiment with lighting, angles, props and anything else you can imagine."

- AMY BUTLER

QUESTION *and* ANSWER
DAVID BUTLER
artofthemidwest.com • photographer / designer

DOES PHOTOGRAPHY PLAY AN EVEN LARGER ROLL IN BRAND PROMOTION THAN IT DID TEN YEARS AGO? WHAT HAS CHANGED?

DAVID BUTLER: I think the only thing that's changed, relevant to the industry, is the need to captivate someone's attention with more humanity and grace—to calm them down instead of hype them up. The internet has clearly changed our perceptions and our levels of patience, not to mention our editorial processes for any type of data. That's been a major factor in the last ten years. There is simply so much put forth to garner attention, that it becomes more important to treat people with an overall feeling that they are taking part in something artistic, not being sold. We've always felt this is what our friends and customers deserve. They deserve to be inspired, to have art in their lives. It should feel fresh and unique, and it should help people to feel comfortable with what you are doing. A good brand tells a story through how it is handled every single photo and effort along the way. Consistency is key to maintaining comfort and keeping people inspired. If it's not fresh and exciting for us, it probably won't be for our friends and customers.

WHAT GOES INTO A STRAIGHTFORWARD PRODUCT SHOT AGAINST WHITE?

DB: My biggest "secret" (which is no secret at all) is that I only use natural light. I have a couple of reflectors and I use white foam core to bounce light around the subject and remove shadows. It's very guerilla. The hardest part is I'm reliant on good natural light, and in Ohio that can be a waiting game! Otherwise I'm just using a Canon EOS 7D camera with a Canon 18-135mm EF-S lens. I have a few other lenses, but almost never use them.

WHAT'S THE DIFFERENCE BETWEEN AN OK PRODUCT SHOT AND A HIGH QUALITY PICTURE?

DB: Color and form. A great image gets the best angle on a shape and the most natural feel of the materials and light.

CAN YOU EXPLAIN POST-PRODUCTION? HOW MUCH GOES INTO A CLIENT'S PHOTOS BEFORE THEY ARE PRINT-READY?

DB: Depending on the shoot, it goes from nothing at all to plenty of time in Aperture and/or Photoshop. Shooting an interior might need tweaking lights and darks in certain areas. Some models may have a few blemishes to cover up. But I really try and keep my post down to a minimum. A vast majority of what I consider to be post is in editing. I take a crazy amount of photos instead of spending too much time on one shot and shooting brackets on a tripod. I'd rather give myself options, moving around and hand holding the camera as much as I can. Of course light restrictions change all of that. Only later do I edit down to the best.

WHAT'S THE MOST COMMON MISTAKE WHEN SHOOTING YOUR OWN PRODUCT?

DB: Probably over styling the shot. I've worked with clients who feel the "product must be perfect" and so the stylist is bending over backwards to make everything seem flawless. That's great if you are shooting a car on a seamless backdrop. But in home interiors and most home products, you need to have a sense of "lived in" in order to allow customers to see themselves in the picture. It's not as easy as it sounds. There is such a thing as "too sloppy" also. But depending on the setting, anything can work. It just needs to be inviting. Styling is super important, I cannot stress enough how a great stylist is worth their weight in gold.

WHAT DO YOU THINK EDITORS ARE LOOKING FOR?

DB: Creativity and unique voice. Uniqueness is key. Our approach matches that of editorial. We try to tell little stories and set moods with our own images, and so editors find that the photos we provide are "ready to go" which is a big factor in having timely releases.

WHAT KIND OF EXPERIENCE SHOULD SOMEONE LOOK FOR WHEN HIRING A PHOTOGRAPHER?

DB: That's pretty easy. Make sure they've shot other things like what you are requesting and see how they've done it in their portfolio. If they haven't, don't be their guinea pig. They might be a fresh art student but if they have the portfolio to back it up then you simply have to point and say— yep, this!

> *"A good brand tells a story through how it is handled every single photo and effort along the way."*
>
> -DAVID BUTLER

six

EDITORS, BLOGGERS & INFLUENCERS

It always surprises me how many well-informed people with a great product have no idea *who* to pitch or *how* to find the right editor to present their idea. And so, it almost always ends there, with people assuming they need a publicist to make that introduction. Finding the right editor or writer and their contact information will take some effort on your part, but you can do it! What's more, editors want to be found (after all, other than going to markets and scouring blogs, this is how they find new material). But it's important to understand that editors want to be approached in a way that gives them the space to make the best decision for the pages and issue they are working on. This means presenting your pitch like the pros with a personable, tightly focused idea, as discussed in Chapter Three. The homework it takes on the front end—finding the right editor and getting their contact information— can pay off mightily when you land national press.

READING THE MASTHEAD

You should think of the masthead as your point of entry to deciphering who's who in magazine production, a map to all of the people you need to contact to get your story published. For every issue there are usually two mastheads, publishing and editorial, and these pages are buried in the front of the magazine between advertisements. Editors and photographers who develop content are generally listed on the editorial masthead. These are the people who shape the stories, write the articles and decide the pictures that run alongside them. The advertising, sales, consumer and marketing staff will be listed on the publishing masthead. These are the people who sell advertising and handle the magazine's finances.

IDENTIFYING THE PROPER EDITOR

Assuming you've read the magazine or online publication and found a section where you think your story or product belongs, does it matter who you approach? Absolutely! There are different editors for almost every section of a publication and then additional editors for the content of the online component of that same publication. If you just guess and send your pitch to the first editor on the masthead, it is time wasted. You have to put it in the hands or the inbox of the editor who pulls together the page you want to see your product on. Editors are bombarded with inquiries. A scattershot mailing or blanket pitch is the easiest email for an editor to delete.

The only time I recommend calling an editorial office (unless you are returning a call from an editor) is to verify the editor of the section you want to pitch so that your idea receives proper consideration. For every section of a magazine there is an editor who produces it, so you may have ten or more different editors pulling the entire magazine together. You want to make sure you pitch the right editor.

It's also important to remember that these pages are generally produced six to seven months in advance for national magazines and three to four months in advance for regional publications. There's always a chance that editors could have moved on or even been promoted to a different position or section in the time between production and print. The success of a pitch is in the timing and targeting. One placement can generate sales and residual interest and is worth the effort it takes to put it in the right hands.

BEFORE REACHING OUT TO AN EDITOR OR BLOGGER YOU SHOULD:

Read more than one issue of the magazine and the most recent blog posts.

———

Study the publication to see if they even cover the type of product or idea you are pitching and to get a feel for their content and tone. There's nothing worse for an editor than receiving a story idea that has little or nothing to do with her last twenty columns.

———

Understand that editors are working six to seven months in advance for national magazines and three to four months for regional publications. Editors may be lounging poolside in June and July or in flip-flops at the farmer's market, but they have holiday gift guides on their mind. Anticipate these themes, then plug in your idea.

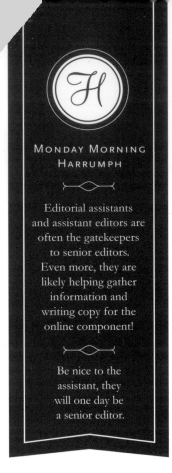

Given that pages are often produced half a year in advance there is any number of reasons why the name of the editor you see on the pages of a current issue is not the editor of that same page now. Follow this step-by-step guide to finding out who to address your pitch.

Step 1: Identify the name of the page or section of the magazine you want to be a part of. Most magazines list them at the top of the page or in the table of contents.

Step 2: Locate the editorial masthead in the front of the magazine.

Step 3: Find the name of an editorial assistant on the masthead. Be sure not to confuse an editorial assistant with an assistant editor, who is higher up on the editorial chain of command. An editorial assistant is an entry-level position, someone who answers phones and supports other editors and is the one person it is ok to phone. If there is no editorial assistant listed, look for an intern.

The majority of national magazines are published under the following four publishers. To access the specific magazine editorial office you must first call the publisher's switchboard operator who will then direct your call. These numbers are never easy to find when you need them, so I have gathered them for you here.

Condè Nast	212-286-2860
Hearst	212-767-6000
Time	212-522-1212
Meredith	515-284-3000

Bloggers generally post their email contact on their site. But one great way to find and reach out to freelance writers, whose names may not be listed on the masthead, is simply by reading the About section of a blog or even searching the name of the author of a writer credited on the page. You may turn up a personal website with a direct contact.

Step 4: Call the editorial office. For most magazines, this means you will call the switchboard to the publisher and ask to be directed to the editorial assistant at the magazine you are pitching. Some editorial office phone numbers are listed at the very bottom of the masthead.

Step 5: Tell the editorial assistant that you have a pitch for the section of the magazine called, for example, "New Designer," and that you want to make certain you get it in front of the right editor for those pages. Ask her to confirm the contact name and the email address of that editor.

Step 6: Thank her politely.

Step 7: Prepare your pitch.

LOLLY POP!

The "face" of the magazine who oversees all editorial activity but not the one making day-to-day editorial decisions.

Reports to the Editor-in-Chief and supervises editorial staff.

Composes feature content and oversees freelance assignments.

Reports to the senior editors and writes smaller sections; often in the front of the magazine.

Future senior editor but the one person it is ok to ask help direct you to the proper editor.

Scouts the market for new products.

EDITOR-IN-CHIEF
Sandy Lou
CREATIVE DIRECTOR
Jennifer Lynn
EXECUTIVE EDITOR
Eric Hendrix
DEPUTY EDITOR
Amy Jean
MANAGING EDITOR
Sara Evans

Features
SENIOR EDITORS
Stephanie Cann, Lindsay Free
ASSISTANT EDITOR
Janet Miller
EDITORIAL ASSISTANTS
Nick Shay, Wilma Smith

Style
STYLE EDITOR
Alissa Hammer
MARKET EDITORS
June Flower (fashion)
Sasha Cohen (home)

Photography
**DIRECTOR
OF PHOTOGRAPHY**
Paul Helman
**ASSOCIATE PHOTO
EDITOR**
Mike Gram
**ASSISTANT PHOTO
EDITOR**
Linda Cole

Art & Production
DESIGNER
Mike Daily
PRODUCTION MANAGER
Hailey Smith
**ASSISTANT MANAGING
EDITOR/ COPY CHIEF**
Danielle Miller
COPY EDITOR
Amy Lucas
RESEARCH EDITORS
Elana Fisher, Adam Silver

WEST COAST EDITOR
Dave Emerson

CONTRIBUTING EDITORS
Kelly Anderson, Amy Atkinson,
Gavin Belk, Lanna Clancy,
Kristine Hackett, Dave Levy,
Catherine Martin, Carol Schmidt

INTERNS
Suzie DeGroff, Tanja Nicolino,
Lester Reed

EDITORIAL OFFICE
Lolly Pop! 555 Lolly Pop Lane,
Atlanta, GA 30308
555-555-1234

Future editorial assistant.

seven

STRATEGY, SYSTEMS & STAMINA

With great photos in place, the impulse to dash off a quick pitch is tempting. You're ready for those long-awaited results! But wait! Do you have a strategy for your next three months? Six months? A year? Do you have a system in place to keep up with what you send out, your follow up and their response? Are samples at the ready for when the editor asks you to send the product you've pitched?

Impulse marketing is one of the most common mistakes people make when reaching out to press. Darting off ideas that are not fully thought out read exactly that, like a half-baked pitch that will need a lot more work on the part of the editor to get it to a place where it might work. Brainstorm with a friend, not an editor, and make sure your pitch is well developed before you hit the send button.

Then make sure that you are prepared when the editor responds, "Yes!" They want to write up your story!

A placement in a national magazine or on a popular site can generate a flood of response or ripple effect of interest from other media outlets. But here is a situation I've seen all too many times. A designer gets the biggest break of their new career with a popular online site like Daily Candy or Refinery 29. Then the day their story is featured, the deluge of interest and traffic crash the site, meaning the readers try to visit but are turned away. All systems down. Today, these larger operations do a better job of preparing their subjects for the attention. And because they have larger editorial staffs, they have longer lead times from production to an article going live in order to prepare.

But a popular blogger or website with a smaller staff may discover a product one day and introduce it to thousands of readers the next. Before sending out even your first pitch, be sure that your host site can handle a crowd. For every designer or company who was ready for their big moment, another budding business missed an opportunity and turned away thousands of potential clients. You don't want to be one of them.

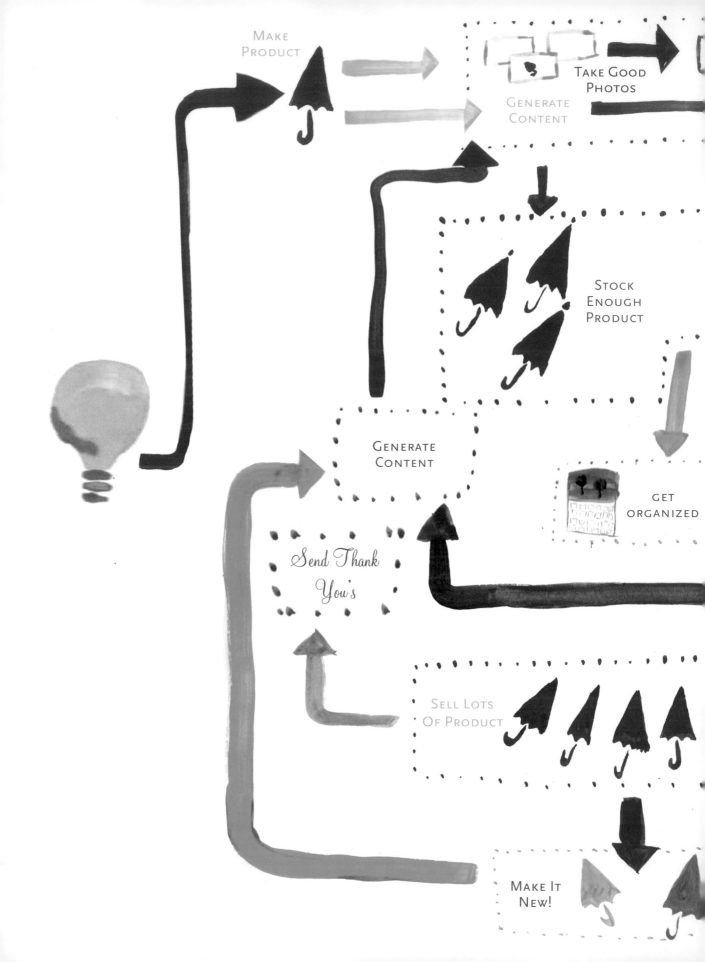

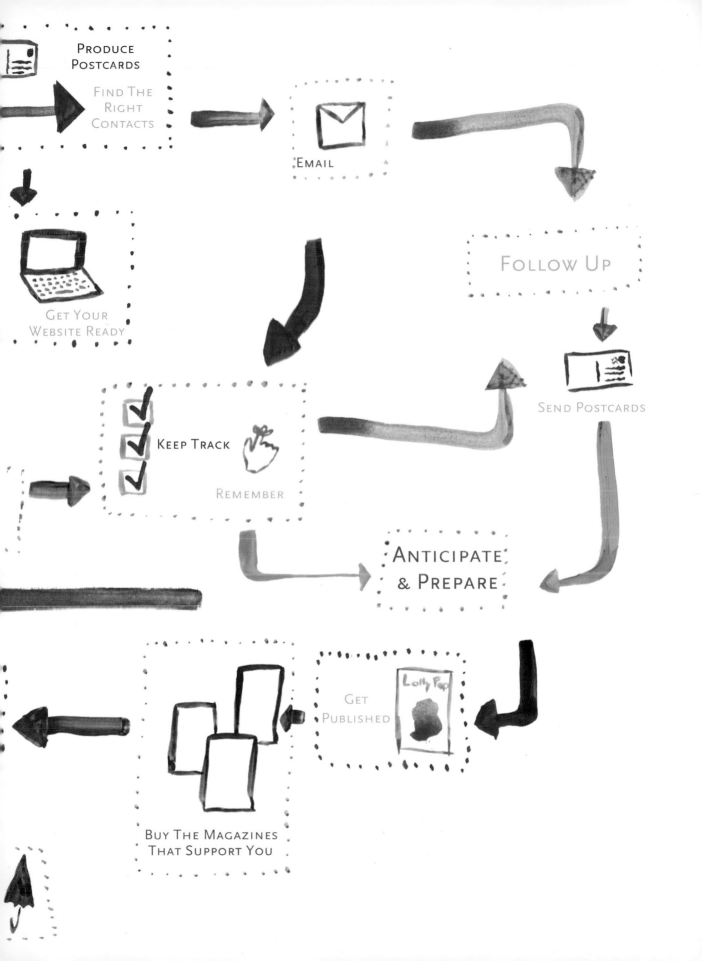

SPREADSHEETS

An effective plan is one that breaks down the process into attainable timelines and goals. Keeping a constant flow of ideas in front of editors and charting follow-up takes stamina and a well-organized system.

Spreadsheets and personal calendar applications like iCal and Google Docs are free, easy to create and can be shared. When the goal is to keep a number of articles featuring or mentioning your company in a variety of publications at all times, you need a way of tracking who you pitched, when you sent it and what the editor responded.

If an editor assigns and subsequently publishes an article in a magazine, then you need to note the stand date or the month it comes out so that you can remember to purchase it. Often ideas are pitched to online editors or bloggers and they publish it right away. Remember to read or at least check the blogs you pitch.

Spreadsheets should also be created to keep track of the comings and goings of writers and editors. Note their contact information and changes both personal and professional that help you connect with them in a meaningful way. Pitch ideas they may gravitate towards based on what you read on their blog and articles they've authored in the past. You want to attract media that makes sense to your product, and you want to give editors the confidence that you are prepared for attention when it comes your way.

I IS FOR IMPLEMENTATION

Sometimes the hardest thing in the world about being your own publicist is, actually, working tirelessly like a good publicist. Very little happens without great effort, consistency and follow-up.

For many small businesses, the biggest hurdle is designating someone to this new communication's position part or full time, especially when it may appear that employee is just reading blogs, sending emails and chit-chatting with friends all day.

But a true understanding of your market and where you belong in it takes constant reading, writing and communicating with various influencers. Possibilities for press are unearthed by listening to others in this larger public conversation and thinking creatively about ways to contribute.

The best person for this job must have good writing skills, be an easy communicator and already an active participant with social sites like Twitter, Pinterest, Tumblr and Facebook. If they are a new hire, part of their training may be to work in various roles within the company before they assume their position in communications. They need to become well-versed enough on the company's philosophy and understanding of boundaries in order to establish a "voice," which requires some level of authority and autonomy.

Some of the most celebrated brand bloggers were already working for that company before being plucked for this new role. If you transition a current employee into this new position, make sure you aren't just tacking this onto their other job. Getting publicity and seeding your message is an invaluable way to grow, but that takes time.

Companies must internalize the fact that in-house marketing and PR is a very important role. In fact, if you don't have this in place five years from now, your company likely won't be around. Success will follow the time put in to the job. Creating structure, even giving the position a title, will help fortify the role in the minds of other employees until efforts can prove that free publicity is a very real avenue to sales. The main thing, however, is that you, the CEO, must believe it!

Send a thank you note to the writer when they include you in an article and comment positively online. Acknowledging the time and thought that went into sharing your story goes a long way toward building a relationship.

eight

GENERATING
CREATIVE CONTENT

There is a pivotal moment midway into my seminars where I recognize the distressed stares of attendees who are clearly overwhelmed with the work cut out for them. Where will they find the time or resources to create enough original content for blogs, mailers, newsletters and social media sites?

With so many ways to reach your audience, one of your greatest challenges may be in finding the time to create fresh and captivating content. How do you keep up this pace without feeling like you're on a roller coaster ride constantly on the verge of derailing?

Rebecca Wood, owner of R. Wood Studio, the largest independent ceramic studio in the southeast, was one of the first business owners I know to embrace the blurring line of lifestyle and business and use it to promote her company as well as those of her friends. It was a concept well ahead of her time. Instead of letting her growing need for editorial-style content become a burden, she treated it as an opportunity to share inspirations with her customers and friends and to keep them engaged not just in the product, but in the brand.

"*Make beauty, inspire each other, photograph it all. That's our motto.*"
- REBECCA WOOD
owner, R. Wood Studio • rwoodstudio.com

"We had so many ideas that we thought editors would love and that our collectors would also enjoy seeing but an even greater urge to share them. We finally decided to just do it ourselves."
-REBECCA WOOD, of her online magazine, beautyeveryday.com

"Ten years ago me and some of the creatives working at R. Wood thought it would be cool to journal online about the things that inspire us, in particular the beauty around the South that informs our art," says Rebecca. "We had so many ideas that we thought editors would love and that our collectors would also enjoy seeing and an even greater urge to share them. We finally decided to just do it ourselves."

As technology caught up with their idea, they created an online magazine called *Beauty Everyday* (beautyeveryday.com). Rebecca divvied up the responsibility of creating content with two other employees whose aesthetic jibed with her own. Studio photographer Rinne Allen, office manager Kristen Bach and Rebecca acted as the backbone of her editorial team.

Ten years later and with the demands from bloggers, writers and editors for lifestyle images at an all-time high, Rinne, a photographer now with her own photography business (rinneallen.com), and Kristen, owner of Treehouse Kid & Craft (treehousekidandcraft.com), still contribute to Beauty Everyday as well as maintain their own blogs and websites. To keep up with it all, they came up with a system that helps them to generate enough fresh content without feeling overwhelmed. Personally, I think it's brilliant.

"We set aside a day every quarter to come together and make beautiful things," says Rebecca. "Kristen is usually in the kitchen whipping up something delicious and seasonal for the food component of the blog and Rinne arranges floral compositions from cuttings from her garden and the meadow. I set up vignettes that we might use as product shots for the web or for postcards. Later, we set a picnic table and eat and catch up. But we are photographing each step. It's like a retreat, but with a purpose."

In that time they generate enough new images to pad three to four months of blogging, Facebook posts, mailers and updates. The friends maintain their posts on Beauty Everyday, making sure the information is constantly updated, enticing readers to come back, to be active participants in the growing R. Wood community. But other pictures are used as filler for the personal blogs as well.

I spent the day with Rebecca, Rinne and Kristen at their spring shoot at Wood's home in Athens, Georgia. Built in 1936, the clapboard structure with an all-pine interior was a former all-black schoolhouse. According to Wood it was fully integrated by 1954 and later saved from dereliction when it became a juke joint. Rays of sunshine streaming through the front windows dapple the rich wood walls and set the backdrop for a day of staging ideas that had been germinating since their last get-together. Both new mothers with active lives, Rinne and Kristen value the aspect of committing time to bring these projects to life as much as the time together with Rebecca.

"*It's like a retreat, but with a purpose.*"

-KRISTEN BACH

"Doing it together is a load off. There is no end to our ideas, but being accountable to each other and to a date helps to see they get done."

- RINNE ALLEN

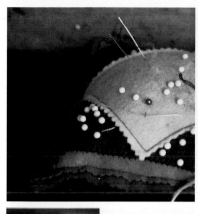

TREEHOUS
kid & craft

⚓

children's shop and DIY ce

kristen bach   owner
kenneth kase   manager

815 west broad street, suite a
athens, ga 30601
706.850.8226
treehousekidandcraft.com
treehousekidandcraft@gmai

caroline petters
photography

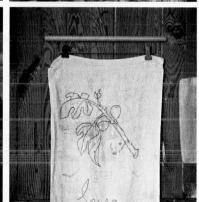

"Getting together every quarter
means the changes of the seasons
will be reflected in our photographs."

-KRISTEN BACH

nine

THE HUMBLE POSTCARD

ALABAMA
CHANIN

A compelling picture that communicates the essence of the brand— and introduces
a new product— is often just the battery to jump-start a story with an editor.

I recommend putting the money you would invest toward creating a press kit into strong product photography, a good camera with a digital video component and website design with an easy-to-operate back-end system. These longer-term marketing materials can be shared the world over with the click of a mouse and make a good case for investing your money differently.

The key elements that once comprised a traditional press kit—the bio, clippings of previous press, a catalog of products—should all be reflected on your website anyway. And this is where editors prefer to go to see and consider your work.

So how then do you get editors to visit your site and consider your story? Email is now an acceptable and preferred way to pitch and introduce a product or idea, as discussed in Chapter Three. But for following up an email query, for personal notes to editors or simply to keep brand presence and awareness in front of a writer, the oversized postcard is one of the most effective and economical marketing tools out there. An oversized postcard with a crisp, clean image on the front of a new product—whether that product is a new book, a new dress collection, or a new logo— is a great way to maintain brand awareness with an editor without bugging them. Think strategically. A beautiful postcard is something an editor can hang on to or pin to her inspiration board, rather than throwing it away. Editors will often keep a postcard until they find a place for the idea in their pages. Sometimes it's just enough of a reminder to spur an idea. Even more often the editor is on deadline and your card signals something "new" they can use immediately.

One well-lit product against a clean white backdrop is a great way to showcase a standout piece and entice an editor to look at the rest of your company's offerings on the website. An image that incorporates the product into a more styled setting can plant the seed and give an editor an idea of how they might use the piece in their magazine. An oversized 5x7 postcard will hold its own in the mail (versus a wimpy 4x6) and won't get lost if tacked up on an inspiration board. Writing a short note on the back suggesting what you have in mind (because you're thinking like an editor, right?) or simply introducing yourself is a great way to get your message across. It's respectful of the editor's time and space but it's also personal.

Keep a number of different oversized postcards at your ready (and remember, they take a regular stamp). If you introduce an orange umbrella to a current collection as a new color, for example, send that postcard in spring and suggest that it might be a great product to consider for an October product roundup (Halloween!) when they are developing fall issues. Great photographs will always catch an editor's eyes. If you choose to style a shoot, just make sure the end result looks at home on the blog or in the magazine you hope to be featured in.

Your web address should be prominently featured on the front or back of the postcard. If editors are stirred by the image, they will go directly to the website or even reach out on the spot. Make sure vitals can be found at a glance.

Printing a series of postcards for each collection and then targeting a variety of editors with the different looks and ideas stretches coverage and ensures that everyone's not wanting to run the same image at the same time.

ten

SAMPLES, GIFTING & GIVEAWAYS

It is not uncommon for a blog to charge for the space on their site in addition to giving away products to readers. So you may end up paying the blogger to host your giveaway and footing the cost of the actual giveaway. This is entirely up to the editor of site or magazine but should not be confused for editorial, which should always be free.

The primary benefit of giveaways for a company or brand is the chance to build your database and reach a target demographic. But you want to get the most out of a giveaway. Here's what you need to remember.

There is room for questions and some bargaining on your end with the editor. If you are the designer behind a swimwear label, for example, and asked to contribute 25 of your best-selling summer suits for a giveaway of summer totes packed with the hottest beach essentials, it is perfectly acceptable to ask what other brands will be represented alongside yours. If they are not on-brand for your company, then you should question if the expense is worth the return.

Seasoned labels familiar with the pros and cons of giveaways know to ask if there can be an opt-in box. An opt-in box is a space where people can add their name and email address to your list to receive more information. Companies are catching on that building a list of email subscribers is one of the most valuable online assets. If the editor cannot promise an opt-in box, ask if they can, at the very least, include a link to your website. There is no one-size-fits-all approach to the giveaway and most editors will work with brands to make the giveaway beneficial to everyone.

Also, be sure you decide before signing a contract who is responsible for fulfilling the orders and for shipping costs. If you're giving away 1000 beauty products and you're also handling shipping expenses, it is a much larger cost to your company than just the product giveaway. Be pleasant and flexible and understanding of the fact that editors generally have another editor or two over them whose deadlines they must meet. Once you and the editor come to an agreement, sign and return papers quickly. Often the thing that gives one company an advantage over the next in securing giveaway placements is the simple fact that they get back to the editor when they say they will.

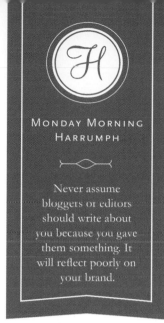

THE ETIQUETTE OF GIFTING

There are times when sending a gift to a writer or editor as a thank you is perfectly appropriate and a fine idea, as long as the gift comes after the article has been posted. Editors appreciate being remembered and getting to share in good news.

A gift to an editor should be thoughtful, but not necessarily expensive. An editor or writer should never feel they are expected to reciprocate with some sort of future post because of something you sent them. A pound of coffee beans from a neighborhood roasting company or a box of pretty colored macaroons from a hip new shop are sweet sentiments without stepping out of bounds. But a hand-written thank you card is always appropriate and goes just as long a way toward establishing a relationship.

Excessive gifting, however, is unnecessary and can put a writer or editor in the uncomfortable position of creating a false sense of expectation. Magazine staffs and bloggers who operated in "freebies" for promise of placement, an ethical maelstrom, do exist. They often tell brands or advertisers how it works with a wink and a nod over lunch.

Don't give in to anyone who suggests "freebies" in order for them to write about you. The best and most influential blogs are built on a trusted voice, influenced by things they choose.

FINDING
YOUR VOICE

If your knee-jerk reaction to industry verbiage like "search optimization," "content catalysts" and "social media tribes" ties your stomach, take a deep breath. The paradigm shift from traditional PR of old to the new "online community" doesn't have to be as weird or corporate a transition as it may sound. In fact, the foundation of new media is really based on an old-fashioned, small business archetype… only with new tools.

The ideal for brands today is to live as part of a conversation on the cyber and sidewalk and to establish a sincere, trusted voice from within the business, not an outside agent. But participating in Twitter, Facebook, Tumblr, Pinterest, and all of the new communicating outlets can, for many small businesses, feel too much to start all at once. Sometimes picking the one that makes sense to you for now and doing it well is the trick to becoming more familiar and comfortable in this new landscape and to developing your brand's voice. From there you can build on what you will learn to be true: that the more you participate in these branding tools, the larger you can grow your audience.

MEET KARA LARSON

After being consistently stopped on the street to ask where she found her dresses, designer Kara Larson started selling them out of the trunk of her vintage Falcon wagon. That was twenty years ago. She didn't have a degree in fashion design and, for that matter, she didn't even give her dresses sizes. Instead, the budding entrepreneur preferred an intuitive fit to her styles that also accommodated the different and creative ways women liked to wear them.

She helped women find "their" dress. Sometimes she even named a style after them. As business picked up, Kara held her dress sales in a garage that, for the weekend, became a stall of fantastical style and ambiance. Women who shopped the makeshift market were there as much for the experience and social time (Kara in her girly, layered prints and scuffed up cowboy boots serving lemonade and licorice) as they were for the shopping.

When the denim craze hit in the early 90's, Kara intensified her campaign, Wear More Dresses! and in 2000 opened Tumbleweed boutique in the Alberta Arts District of Portland, Oregon.

Today Tumbleweed and Grasshopper, her children's shop next door, are thriving amidst the languishing retail landscape that has closed so many specialty doors.

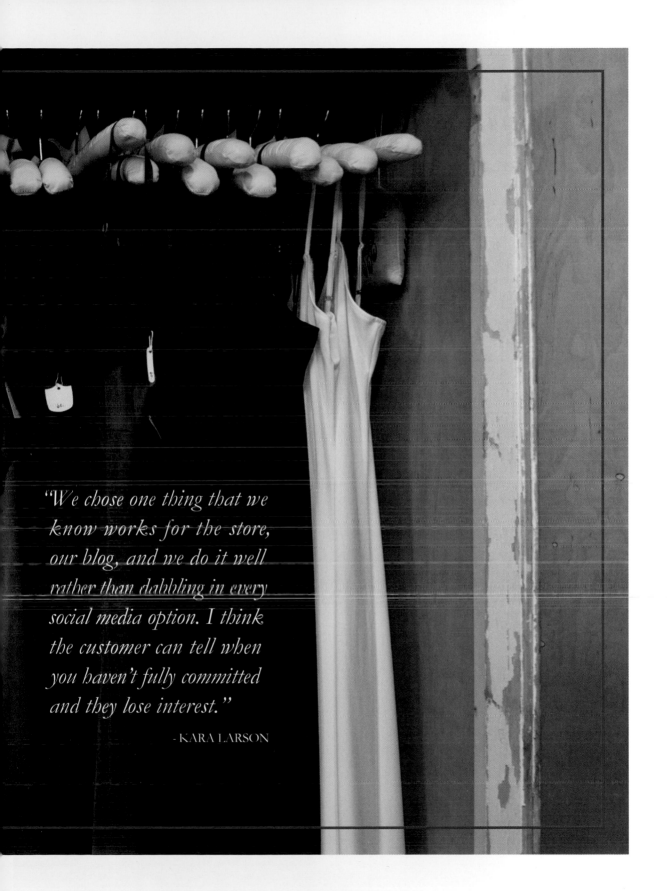

"We chose one thing that we know works for the store, our blog, and we do it well rather than dabbling in every social media option. I think the customer can tell when you haven't fully committed and they lose interest."

- KARA LARSON

tumbleweedboutique.typepad.com

"At the end of the day, it's a story people love. People still talk about how I used to sell my dresses out of the back of my car. It's more charming and people feel like they know me."

-KARA LARSON
kara-line.com

How? For starters she added more staples under her own label, Kara-line, keeping production local as she always had and in small runs that she was sure she could sell. She also put added emphasis on customer service. "That's always been important, but we looked for new ways to retain their loyalty," she says.

Kara does not have a Twitter account and when asked about Facebook she wrinkles her nose before admitting that, if she has one, she doesn't remember how to sign in. To the dismay of editors everywhere, she refuses to offer e-commerce, instead opting for a collaborative commerce system of sending boxes of options to distant clients who pay for what they love and send the rest back. "Selling a dress online takes away the personal touch," she says. "Anyone can look at a dress and go 'oh, I love it,' but it may not be right for their body. So we have an old-school form that we ask people to fill out before sending out a box. Ninety percent of the time we really know what a customer will love and look best in even though we've never met!"

What, then, is to account for the uptick in sales when so many boutiques barely detect a pulse? "Our blog," she says. "It has catapulted sales."

Long a technology holdout, Kara simply discovered the right platform— the blog— to share her story. And in doing so she discovered an enormous and appreciative community (and new clients!) outside the walls of her store.

Still, there was a learning curve to getting that right, to learning exactly what her customers were looking for in the posts. "My first attempt was called 'diary of a designer' and it was a more personal thing, like what I was growing in my garden or where I was eating," says Kara. "The problem was that I would forget to post and I just wasn't consistent enough to really engage readers. And it wasn't the best business strategy either, directing focus on me, instead of the store."

So Kara and her team shifted the focus to what was going on inside Tumbleweed, giving readers the scoop on new arrivals and finding ways to make that personal.

"When we turned the attention back onto the store, activity on the blog spiked!"

According to Kara, blogging makes business more exciting, both for her and her staff and her customers. "We've always ordered limited runs of styles and fabrics to keep our stock fresh and our Portland shoppers know this and love that they have part of a small collection," she says. "Our readers know that if they do not contact us within a week of something posted, it will be gone. So as soon as we put new pictures up, the phones start ringing. It's nuts, but it feels good."

"Customers are really looking to feel like they're a part of our day, even when they can't come into the boutique. So we keep things personal and local but with an emphasis on product." Kara Larson, of this recent blog post, *Dear sweater fairy, If you feel like visiting shop gal, Susan, in the middle of the night, she wouldn't be offended if you left this sweater under her pillow...*

twelve

PREPARING FOR THE INTERVIEW

*I*t's flattering when a writer requests an interview or responds positively to a pitch. Part of the joy for writers is also in delivering the good new and sharing in your excitement!

Before you get together, however, take time to read some of their past articles. Just as the writer will research your brand story before the interview, you should also familiarize yourself with their style. How has the writer portrayed past subjects? Even if you only have the time to read a few articles, make it a priority. By studying their work style, you'll be more aware of the story you should present and complimenting a favorite article is also a positive way to segue into your interview and establish the tone.

But there are other important reasons for doing your homework and treating the writer and their time with the same respect you hope to receive.

CONTROLLING YOUR STORY

I once had the opportunity to interview designer Vera Wang, having been assigned to write a feature on her for a luxury lifestyle magazine. In arranging the interview, the designer's in-house publicist asked that I submit my questions in advance, a practice typical of seasoned celebrities and high-profile businesspeople able to get away with those demands. With no choice, I sent my eight questions. A day later, her publicist requested that I whittle the list down to my top three.

Frankly, I was miffed, even a little insulted. I questioned the logic in their wanting me to write a feature if my subject were only willing to answer three questions?

But in researching and preparing my questions, I spent a lot of time on her backstory and on frequently asked questions. And that helped me to shape three solid questions that would make my story different, give it focus and perhaps open up a larger discussion. And it did. The designer was thoughtful in her response and generous with her time and didn't stray from the story with unnecessary babble.

It was a valuable lesson. By insisting on preparation and brevity, She ensured that both her time and my own was not wasted.

I am not suggesting that everyone can pull such a diva stunt without distancing yourself from the writer early on, but there's something to learn in valuing both your and the writer's time.

Open-ended interviews without any sense of order or expectation set both you and the writer up for disappointment. Publicity can come at a price.

Take, for example, the artist who shared some of her poor health issues during an interview, a subject completely off-topic of the reason for the interview: the launch of her pottery line. "The writer was so friendly and conversation naturally wove in and out of all kinds of topics, including my health," she said. "When the article came out, the first sentence reported that I had been a sick child, an area I really thought was off limits. I couldn't even finish the article, I was so upset."

Both examples are testaments to why asserting some kind of control, even if it's simply by putting time limits on interviews, is critical.

From the outset, there are two goals going into any interview: those of the reporter and your own. By thinking of what you want to communicate before you get together will help you maintain your purpose and even lead it back around if conversation strays.

Email interviews give you the space and luxury of thinking about answers to questions. But if a writer insists on getting together, be available and approachable, generous, but guarded. Understand also that unless you predicate an antidote or joke or nugget of information you would rather not share with the world that, "this is off the record," it's fair game to the writer and can be included in the article. And by all means, don't put a competitor down or bad-mouth another area writer. Nothing positive ever comes out of loose-lipped inferences.

Communication today thrives on transparency; little seems to be off limits. But with practice and good communication, you and your team will grow more confident and comfortable in sharing freely when you know your purpose and parameters.

MONDAY MORNING
HARRUMPH

Don't ask the journalist to send you a few copies of the magazine that featured your story. They are rarely, if ever, sitting on stacks of the publication and they would appreciate your purchasing the magazine that supported you!

FACT CHECKING

Sometimes, writers may offer to let you review a paragraph or section of the article before they turn it into their editor, particularly when dealing with sensitive material or unfamiliar waters. But no self-respecting writer will let you read the story before it goes to print, so refrain from asking.

If you feel that you failed to mention something critical during the interview, don't wait to reach out. Send an email soon after your interview and keep it brief.

If the writer has follow-up questions, be sure to respond to their email or call as quickly as possible as they are likely nearing a deadline to turn it in. When the article comes out (and whether or not you are crazy about their approach,) always take the time to reach out and thank the writer for the time spent on sharing your story. If you're happy with it, post the story on Facebook, Tweet the link, brag on the writer, spread the word freely. A little love goes a long way and may even result in a second or third story on your product or business down the road.

All too often writers hear only what's wrong with an article. If you're not happy with the article, think before telling the writer. Calling a writer to complain about a story or expressing disappointment in the article length or the lack of response your brand got from the exposure (this does happen) will wreck your relationship. If you feel that an inaccuracy has lead to permanent brand damage, you should ask for a correction or retraction and expect that correspondence be handled professionally on their end as well. Otherwise, keep it positive and upbeat. When something good comes from a placement, editors and writers enjoy knowing they were a part of your success.

thirteen
FOLLOWING UP

Editors, freelance writers and bloggers are generally an amiable bunch and will be your biggest ambassadors if they like what you do and enjoy working with you. Worth reviewing is the communication protocol; while unofficial, these mistakes can have lasting impact on your relationship.

Calling an editor to pitch your story. The only call you should make to an editorial office is to double check the editor's contact information with an assistant.

Asking to read or review the story before it goes to print.

Sending attachments with your pitch. Editors will only open it if they requested the images and then they should be in Jpg format, not pdfs, power points and zip that are easily corrupted via email.

Flooding the same editor with too many ideas at once. It's a lot like asking the teacher to complete your homework. Develop one good idea and personalize it for the publication you're pitching.

Asking an editor if you can have a coffee together to "pick her brain."

Misspelling the editor, writer or blogger's name.

Complaining about the article after it's in print. There are always a number of editors involved in the final decisions. Things like article length and photography do get changed at the last minute and are often out of the control of the writer or editor you worked with.

Neglecting to cross-promote. Communications today is not a flat continuum. If you want to engage with a readership outside of your niche, invite someone you admire to guest blog, offer to guest blog with a brand you love or team up with a publication or blog.

Sending out mass press releases. Tailoring your pitch to writers and bloggers is the right way to foster personal relationships and earn placements.

You've worked hard to pull together a strong pitch and you took the time to get it in the right hands. Now what?

Follow-up is an important component of your outreach and is, quite often, just the reminder an editor needs to actually find a place for your idea in her editorial lineup. And there is a way to do it that will earn you the respect of the editor, not their ire.

Give an editor about ten days before sending a short follow-up via email. You only get one shot so you'll want to remind her in the first sentence of your general pitch idea or product. If you have offered an exclusive on breaking the news or even on a certain angle, mention that too. Ending the paragraph with a question that asks if she sees a place for your story in an upcoming issue is an effective way of getting a response. If she passes on your pitch, by all means, stay positive and thank the editor for the consideration. Remember, a "no" simply means "no for now," and this back and forth is relationship building. The next time you pitch this same editor, you might remind her of the first exchange before launching into another idea that, you feel, is an even better fit.

When it comes to pitching bloggers, it's natural to want to follow up with them too. But bloggers are different. They are working and posting in real time. If they like your idea and find it captivating, they will use it. They may not give you any warning they plan to post it or even let you know when they do (they assume that if you're pitching their blog, you must be following it too). If they can't use it, they won't.

As tempting as it may be, don't resend the same message or inquire if a blogger received it or ask if they plan to include it. The only thing you'll succeed in is in running them off. Simply send a thank you after it's posted. If they choose not to run it, remember the "no for now" rule. When you work hard at creating attractive content, you'll eventually win over the blogger and earn their respect for getting it right and not giving up.

fourteen

MAKING IT
AT MARKET

"*If a vendor can tell a story, they'll sell.*"

-SONJA RASULA
founder of UNIQUE LA

*S*onja Basula is the founder of UNIQUE LA, the largest independent design and gift show in the country and the face of a growing Made-in-the-USA movement. A community-minded Los Angeles native, her career epiphany came in late 2008 after spending most of the year volunteering to register voters.

After the elections, she developed the concept of a large-scale event in Los Angeles that promoted local design. Using her own savings and drawing on the diversity of her work experience as an editor and new media expert, Sonja set out to create a showcase of local and independent design that "rivaled the mall."

Staged in a sleek downtown high-rise with panoramic views of the city, plenty of parking, a food court that serves macrobiotic offerings, specialty cocktails and giveaways galore, UNIQUE LA is the model for the 21st century independent marketplace with over 300 vendors that attract 24,000 shoppers each show.

In addition to expanding into new markets (San Francisco, Toronto and New York), Sonja launched a local food cart equivalent called LA Street Food Fest, which took off so quickly, she rented the Rose Bowl to host the second event. "All along, my motto has been 'go big or go home,'" says Sonja. "In order to contribute to the sustainability of the artists and to educate the masses on buying local— these markets need to attract thousands and thousands. I am passionate about teaching people the worth and value of great design and how buying local supports the local economy."

Sonja Rasula is a community-building juggernaut who knows it takes more than just a good product to stand out in the crowd. Here, she shares what makes a vendor, and a show at this level, successful.

WHAT DIFFERENTIATES A UNIQUE SHOW FROM THE OTHER LARGE MARKETS?

SONJA RASULA: All of the products sold at Unique are Made In the United States. We feature vendors who have made the tough decision to make their goods here in America (not just design them here) and are therefore supporting the US economy.

AND WHAT DISTINGUISHES UNIQUE FROM A MORE TRADITIONAL CRAFT OR ART FAIR?

SR: Other shows introduce people to the idea of craft, which is great, but it is very hard to be a sustainable business on the art of handmade alone. Unique is more about bringing awareness to the idea that a consumer can make a conscious decision to buy local, Made in America, with everything in their life, from clothing to jewelry to toys, not just produce at farmer's markets. And our aesthetic is clean, modern design.

WHO SHOPS THE MARKET, ASIDE FROM LOCALS?

SR: Lots of fashion stylists walk the show and we get people from Disney and Warner Brothers and other studios. We had one T-shirt artist get discovered by a studio here. They loved his artwork so much they ask him to design everything from holiday cards to product. And then, of course, we get a lot of media and store buyers.

WHAT DO YOU LOOK FOR IN A VENDOR APPLICANT?

SR: It really does come down to what they make and if it's a good fit for Unique. But the first thing we look at is their website. For us it's a benchmark for those who understand what they do and understand marketing. The photography needs to be great and the product should speak to our demographic. If we can tell from their website, application and/or Facebook page that they are great business people (not just a great designer or artist) that's very important to us.

WHAT SETS APART THE APPLICANTS WHO GET IN AND THOSE WHO DON'T?

SR: We do our research and see what they've done in the past. If they did a show six months ago and had great signage and branding material, and were prepared to take credit cards, then that's a clue to us that they're not just an artist, but a serious business person which is important to us at Unique. But passion and 'heart' also play a role. If a designer does not have a website but shows us great products and conveys a lot of passion, we pay attention.

HOW IMPORTANT IS GOOD PHOTOGRAPHY?

SR: It's the first impression, so…
These days people are making sure to shoot the product well; they understand lighting and they know to shoot in front of a blank white wall or they style the products well. Applicants who put more work into their photos definitely attract us more.

WHAT INFO DO YOU WANT TO SEE IN AN APPLICATION?

SR: We want to see great design paired with an understanding of sales/marketing (in how the applicant presents their brand). There are many things we look at—including their price point and whether our consumers will respond well to the designs. It's important to do your research, to take five minutes to look at what past vendors have sold, to read our blog.

WHAT QUALITIES DO YOUR MOST SUCCESSFUL VENDORS SHARE?

SR: They are outgoing, they are 'cheerleaders' as opposed to 'Negative/Nervous Nellies,' and they tell their story visually; MNKR out of California does graphic tees and this past market launched their own jewelry line too. The reason they're so successful is because they both come from a retail background and that corporate training has served them really well in knowing how to market to their customer. They have a well-designed booth and bargain bins that draw people into the booth. In addition, they have flags hanging in the backdrop that say *Made in the USA* and they give away stickers and branded items to people whether they buy something or not.

ETYPE SCARF

ELYSE MARKS
DESIGN

CATIRPEL JEW

FINE HANDMADE PRODUCTS

SALE

10% off

15% off

20% off

ASK US ABOUT CUSTOM ORDERS

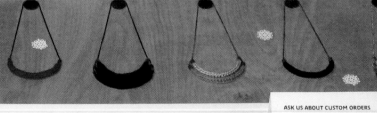

IS IT MORE DIFFICULT FOR LESS EXPERIENCED VENDORS?

SR: Elyse Marks was fresh out of art school and did our show only a few months after graduating. Her success is the culmination of a good simple product, a great personality and a smart presentation of her jewelry. Because Elyse was new, she rented a table over a booth because it was more affordable. But instead of just decorating her table, she built a structure around it. She put time and effort and a lot of thought into doing something different so when shoppers walked by the tables, hers stood out. She almost sold out the first day.

WHEN SOMEONE IS ON THE CUSPS OF BEING ACCEPTED INTO A UNIQUE SHOW, WHAT IS GENERALLY HOLDING THEM BACK?

SR: Usually it is pricing. We know right away if the product fits the show but we also investigate if the applicant's pricing is off with the rest of the market.

Because what sells at the market is made in the United States, we're fine with slightly higher priced items. But, for example, an American Apparel T-shirt with some type of graphic on the front for $70, is not going to sell, even if you've seen it in a boutique for that price. The other thing is usually quantity of product. We have loved some applicants but they only have three designs —with the large amount of shoppers that attend, we know from the past that they aren't ready. But then they apply six months later with more designs, new colorways, male and female sizing and we accept them!

HOW IMPORTANT IS IT TO YOU THAT VENDORS HAVE TWITTER AND FACEBOOK ACCOUNTS?

SR: It's not really something that will come between being accepted, but we do ask if they have a Facebook page or a Twitter feed because if they do we will follow/fan them and can cross promote. My recommendation is that they read up and understand how Twitter can help their business. For me it is a normal thing that has been so integral for growing Unique. Even if you only tweet once a week, it keeps your brand out there, alive.

And Twitter is a great way to attract attention from media. You can now start a dialogue and be a part of an editor's conversation and there's really never been a medium that allowed that to happen before.

DO YOU WORK ON KEEPING UP WITH EDITORS, OR JUST WAIT FOR THEM TO COME TO YOU?

SR: It is so important to maintain those relationships, even if you're only emailing a few times a year. It's more about a relationship to me and then when I'm a good fit, there is no question it will be plugged in. For example, if I know an editor is going on a vacation because they posted it on Twitter, I'll make a point to ask her how it was. I'll send mugs from a show that has passed, just to ask them to mention us the following year. I like to stay on their radar and give them a chance to put us on theirs.

HOW DOES YOUR EXPERIENCE AS AN EDITOR PLAY INTO THIS NEW ROLE AS FOUNDER AND CURATOR?

SR: The experience of being an editor and looking down at a sheet of paper and knowing what to delete without having emotional attachment is a key to properly curating Unique. It's an odd skill, to intuitively know what needs to be added, or what should not be there, or that there's a better way to do this. I know I wouldn't want to go to a show where I wasn't having a great time or that my husband wouldn't enjoy. After walking around our last show I knew we needed to add a second lounge seating area, find more housewares vendors, and offer free water.

This is how I curate and group the vendors in order to make it an interesting show.

WHAT IS UNIQUE'S DEMOGRAPHIC?

SR: It's 55 percent women and 45 percent men and that says something amazing about the team of people at Unique who have created this audience. We know we're doing a great job if men who normally spend Sunday watching football are willing to come and spend hours if not the whole day to shop.

CONCLUSION

Though the steps I've outlined here may seem complicated, the idea behind this book is simple and brings to mind a host of clichés, not the least of which is: there are many things that money can't buy.

You now know that the PR industry exists for a reason. Getting your brand out there and keeping it relevant and in front of your audience takes time, energy, creativity, persistence and passion. At certain levels of success you can pay for some of these, and people do. But unless or until your enterprise gets to that level, paying for a public relations strategy may be outside the realm of possibility. Your success, however, is not.

Cultivating the passion for promoting your brand from within is crucial when the budget for PR campaigns is nonexistent. Deciding who is going to do it is often the most difficult step. Companies with a small staff often feel they are too busy to pull someone off their job to do it and not large enough to have a full-time communication's position.

But ultimately, you have to decide how important this aspect of your business is and how it's going to find a voice. Your story is what differentiates you from the next brand and frankly, no one knows it or shares it better than you. Your challenge as a business today is to create a sustainable strategy that works, that engages your audience to look, listen to your message and then like it enough to share it with others.

It is my goal that *Recipe for Press* serve as a guide, a reference and a training tool for brands who want to grow their PR at their own pace and get it right. Relationships with editors, bloggers and new online influencers who can help put your brand in front of markets far and wide aren't created overnight. From the examples I've shared, you can see it is ongoing and takes a pro-active approach and a well planned strategy. But you can do it and when done correctly, no one will be more effective.

A new level of exposure awaits that can open the doors to more than just a larger audience. There are collaborations and opportunities that will find you only when you put yourself out there.

More than anything, customers have so many choices that if you're not actively promoting your brand and sharing all of the great things you have going on, you'll lose out. Outreach to press should be an important part of your business plan and now you can feel confident that you're going about it correctly. Good luck in getting the word out!

Notes

RECIPE FOR PRESS

The author wishes to thank the following for permission to reproduce their photographs:

Anticipating Stories
Photos by Sarah Dorio

· · · · ·

Power of the Picture
Photos by David Butler

· · · · ·

Generating Creative Content
Photos by Caroline Petters

· · · · ·

The Humble Postcard
Photos courtesy of bla bla kids,
Alabama Chanin and Eva Franco

· · · · ·

Finding Your Voice
Photos by Sherri Diteman

· · · · ·

Making it at Market
Photos by Marat Shaya

· · · · ·

Sonja Rasula profile picture:
Boudoir Rouge Photography

· · · · ·

Picture of Elyse Marks booth:
Courtesy of Elyse Marks

· · · · ·

Amy Flurry profile picture
Photo by Sarah Dorio